ANCIENT CHINESE GOVERNMENT AND GEOGRAPHY

AVERY ELIZABETH HURT

ROSEN
PUBLISHING®

New York

Published in 2017 by The Rosen Publishing Group, Inc.
29 East 21st Street, New York, NY 10010

Copyright © 2017 by The Rosen Publishing Group, Inc.

First Edition

Library of Congress Cataloging-in-Publication Data

Names: Hurt, Avery.
Title: Ancient Chinese government and geography / Avery Elizabeth Hurt.
Description: First edition. | New York : Rosen Publishing, 2017. | Series: Spotlight on the rise and fall of ancient civilizations | Includes
  bibliographical references and index.
Identifiers: LCCN 2016005001| ISBN 9781477789513 (library bound) | ISBN
  9781477788905 (paperback) | ISBN 9781477788912 (6-pack)
Subjects: LCSH: China—Politics and government—To 221 B.C.—Juvenile
  literature. | China—Geography—Juvenile literature.
Classification: LCC DS741.75 .H87 2017 | DDC 931—dc23
LC record available at http://lccn.loc.gov/2016005001

Manufactured in the United States of America

CONTENTS

THE MIDDLE KINGDOM

China is a very big country. If you could pick up all of mainland United States and move it across the world, it would fit inside China. China is bordered by mountains (including the Himalayas), two deserts (the Gobi and the Taklamakan), and the South China Sea.

In ancient times, these mountains and deserts formed a kind of barrier around China. Even now it can be difficult to cross such high mountains and wide deserts, one of which is so dangerous it has been called the sea of death. But before the modern era these barriers meant that China was virtually isolated from the rest of the world.

The people of ancient China knew that there were other tribes of people to the north, but they didn't know that there were other civilizations in faraway places. Chinese people called their country the "Middle Kingdom" because they thought it was the center of the world.

RUSSIA

MONGOLIA

CHINA

Burqin

Ürümqi

Aksu

Bayingol

Jiayuguan

Golmud

Xining

Lanzhou

Naqqu

Lhasa

Xigazê

Nyingchi

Qamdo

NEPAL

BHUTAN

BANGLADESH

MYANMAR

Kunming

Guiyang

Liuzhou

Nanning

VIETNAM

LAOS

THAILAND

Hainan

BAY OF
BENGAL

Andaman
Sea

Zhangye

Wuwei

Yinchuan

Wuhai

Shizuishan

Shuòzhōu

Datong

Yulin

Taiyuan

Yangquan

Yan'an

Guyuan

Tongchuan

Linfen

Yuncheng

Changzhi

Jincheng

Tianshui

Baoji

Xi'an

Hanzhong

Ankang

Mianyang

Nanchong

Chengdu

Neijiang

Chongqing

Changde

Guiyang

Heihe

Hegang

Qiqihar

Jixi

Baicheng

Harbin

Mudanjiang

Changchun

Jilin

Tongliao

Siping

Hunchiang

Chifeng

Shenyang

Fushun

Chaoyang

Benxi

Jinzhou

Anshan

Dandong

Zhangjiakou

Hohhot

Chengde

Baotou

BEIJING

Tangshan

Baoding

Tianjin

Dalian

Shijiazhuang

Cangzhou

Yantai

Dezhou

Binzhou

Weifang

Xingtai

Handan

Jinan

Tai'an

Qingdao

Anyang

Zhengzhou

Zàozhuāng

Lianyungang

Luoyang

Shangqiu

Xuzhou

Nanyang

Suzhou

Huai'an

Taizhou

Fuyang

Huainan

Nanjing

Nantong

Lu'an

Hefei

Wuxi

Wuhu

Suzhou

Shanghai

Jingzhou

Wuhan

Anqing

Hangzhou

Ningbo

Huangshan

Nanchang

Changsha

Hengyang

Fuzhou

Quanzhou

Xiamen

Shantou

Guangzhou

Foshan

Shenzhen

Hong Kong

NORTH
KOREA

SOUTH
KOREA

SEA
OF
JAPAN

JAPAN

Yellow
Sea

EAST CHINA
SEA

TAIWAN

SOUTH
CHINA SEA

PHILIPPINES

Three Gorges Dam

Qinghai
Lake

Hulun Lake

Khanka
Lake

Hung-tse Lake

Dongting
Lake

Heilong Jiang

Amur

Songhua

Yellow

Yangtze

Yangtze

Brahmaputra

Salween

Lancang (Mekong)

Tarim

Aksu

Siling Co

Ngari

Xigazê

China is so big that it contains almost every type of habitat, including alpine
mountains, deciduous forests, vast deserts, and rich, fertile plains.

5

MANY ENVIRONMENTS

China has almost every kind of landscape: wide plains, deserts, mountains, rich river bottoms, and even tropical rain forests. The rivers and mountains of China divide the country into different regions. Each region has a different climate that is good for growing different kinds of crops. It is cold and dry in the north, with a short growing season, but it is also very fertile because of the silt from the rivers. The people of ancient China grew wheat and millet in the north. Most of China's early civilizations developed in the north because the plains of the north were rich and fertile enough to produce food for the growing population. Eventually the people of northern China settled into towns and villages. In southern China, where it is warmer and wetter with a longer growing season, the ancient Chinese people grew rice. Heavy rains during monsoon season make the area perfect for growing rice.

Valleys and plains of northern China, surrounded by mountains, have been home to nomadic tribes for thousands of years.

GREAT RIVERS

China has two major rivers—the Huang He in the north (called the Yellow River in English) and the Chang Jiang (called the Long River in English) in the south. The Chang Jiang is the third longest river in the world. Though much of the country is covered in steep mountains and dry deserts, the rivers that run through the central part of China bring good, fresh water and create fertile floodplains. Though flooding makes the land fertile, it can also be a problem. The Huang He was called China's sorrow because the river flooded so often. It took a great deal of cooperation and organization to control this flooding so that people could live, grow crops, and build cities that would last in this region. The first civilization in China developed in the areas surrounding the Huang He. In English we call it the Yellow River Valley Civilization.

The Chang Jiang flows almost 4,000 miles (6,437 kilometers) across China, from the Tibetan plateau in the west to where it meets the East China Sea near modern-day Shanghai.

TIME OF LEGENDS

The story of Yu the Great and the Great Flood is one of the oldest legends in China. Chinese schoolchildren still learn the story. In ancient times, the legend goes, there was a great flood, and water covered most of the land. Yu the Great worked for thirteen years digging deep rivers to hold the water so that homes would be safe from flooding and farmers could find dry land to plant crops.

The story of Yu is just a legend, and there is no evidence that he ever lived. However, the story is a true one in a way—to build a lasting civilization with enough food and homes for everyone, the people of ancient China had to develop some kind of flood control. There were probably many people like Yu the Great in ancient China, working together to build dams and irrigation systems so that the Yellow River Valley Civilization could flourish.

河伯

Yu the Great tames the flood-waters. Yu was one of the few ancient Chinese rulers to be given the honorary title "the Great."

This early Chinese society is now called the Xia. There are no records from this early period, which lasted from around 6000 to 1500 BCE, because writing had not been invented yet. Most of what we know comes from legends, like the one about Yu, or from writings of later societies. But archaeologists have found bronze implements, tombs, and evidence of cities showing that the Xia did exist. This period was a time when society was transitioning from widely scattered Stone Age villages into more organized and cooperative civilizations. The ruling class of the Xia lived in walled cities. The peasants lived outside the city walls and were farmers. They grew rice and millet, raised chickens and pigs, and raised silkworms to harvest silk. Archaeologists are continually discovering more about the Xia society. It turns out that the story of Yu is probably based on some truth: the Xia had irrigation and a system of flood control.

Tourists visit structures called dagobas, which scholars think may have been built during the Xia dynasty. They lined the bank of the Yellow River in present-day Qingtongxia, China.

THE FIRST DYNASTY

The Xia civilization was organized into family clans, ruled by chieftains. Each chieftain was in charge of a large tribe made up of his extended family. According to the legends, after Yu saved society from flooding, he became the king of all the tribes in the area. When Yu died, he left his kingdom to his son. Tradition tells us that this was the beginning of the Xia dynasty, the first in a series of kingdoms in which rule was handed down from father to son in a single family. Although historians do not know much detail about who the Xia rulers actually were, they do believe that the dynasty system of government started in this period. The written records of the later dynasties indicate that this system had been established long before the time that they were written. The dynastic system of rule that began with the Xia lasted in China for thousands of years.

Scholars learn much about ancient dynasties by studying their tombs, like these imperial tombs of the Western Xia excavated at the foot of the Helan Mountains.

NATURE GODS

Xia people worshipped nature gods such as the river god, the rain god, and the earth god. Like most farming cultures, they valued the agricultural gods most of all, and a spring festival was held each year to celebrate them. The spring festival was an important festival, and it is still celebrated in China today (now it is also called the New Year festival). In ancient times, people prayed to the agricultural gods to protect them from famine and natural disasters. The greatest of all their gods was the sky god, who was in charge of agriculture and the weather, as well as war and government. While not much is known about how the Xia worshipped, it is believed that they didn't call on the sky god directly. They worshipped the spirits of their dead ancestors instead and asked these ancestors to petition the sky god on their behalf. Ancestor worship became very important in later dynasties.

This clay sculpture of an ancient sage is from the Xia dynasty. It is now in a museum in Beijing, China.

KING OF KINGS: THE SHANG DYNASTY

Around 1600 BCE, another kingdom, called the Shang, which had been growing and gaining power, conquered the Xia and began the Shang dynasty of rulers. We know more about the people of the Shang dynasty because they developed writing and left records of their society. Most of what we know about the Shang comes from ox bones and turtle shells! These bones and turtle shells are called oracle bones because the rulers wrote messages and questions on them and used them to ask the spirits of their ancestors for advice and information about the future. The king would carve questions like "How many men should we send into battle?" and "Will the king have a son?" He would then heat the bones until they cracked. Priests would help the king interpret the patterns of the cracks for the answers to his questions. The questions and answers on these oracle bones tell us a lot about the Shang people.

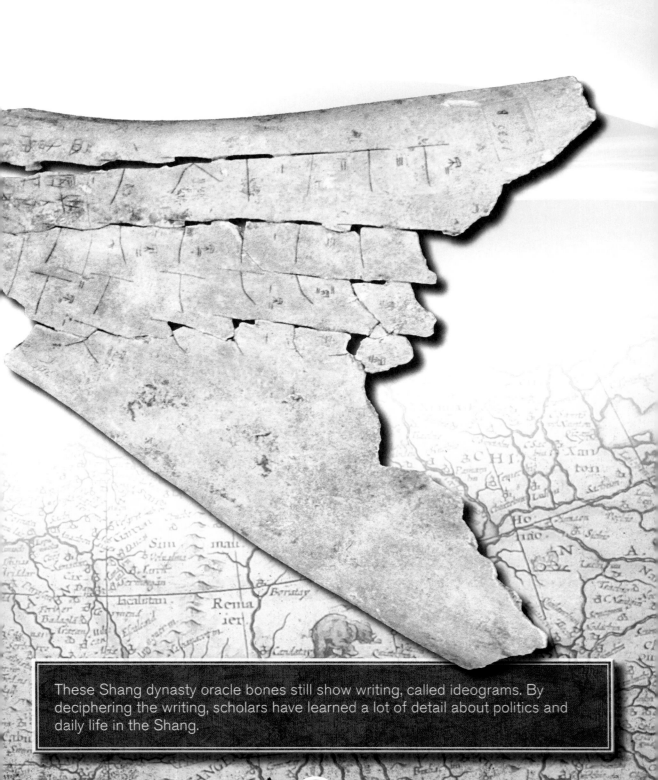

These Shang dynasty oracle bones still show writing, called ideograms. By deciphering the writing, scholars have learned a lot of detail about politics and daily life in the Shang.

The Shang kings and nobles lived in walled cities and commanded large armies. The peasants lived in the surrounding farmlands. Shang society was divided into rigid classes of king, nobles, commoners, and slaves. Shang kings ruled over the smaller family chieftains, and the kingship was often passed from brother to brother or uncle to nephew rather than from father to son.

The Shang dynasty lasted for about six hundred years, during the height of the Bronze Age, when people mined copper and tin ore and combined it to make bronze. They used bronze to make a variety of weapons and implements. The Shang had very large, highly organized armies, some with more than ten thousand soldiers, and they waged many wars on neighboring tribes. They conquered a large territory that at one point covered as much as 40,000 square miles (103,600 sq km) and brought back prisoners who were used as slave labor or as sacrifices to their gods.

This ceremonial axe, dating from the Shang dynasty, is a good example of the intricate metalwork, both practical and ceremonial, produced by Shang artisans.

ROLE OF THE KING

The Shang king was both a political and a religious leader. He was a priest as well as a king and consulted the oracle bones himself or with the help of a lesser priest or shaman. He would intercede with the gods of crops and weather, between the living and dead, and he told the people when it was time to plant and harvest crops. He administered a large and complex government. The Shang government had a hierarchy of jobs with a variety of specializations and many levels of authority. One person might be in charge of building cities, another person might oversee the mining of ore for making bronze, while someone else directed the construction of irrigation systems. Each of these people answered to the king, and many other people answered to them. This hierarchical system of responsibility was a major contribution of the Shang government.

The Shang kings were powerful rulers of a very complex society. Cheng Tang (pictured here) may have been the first king of the Shang dynasty.

DEATH OF THE KING

Besides oracle bones, much of what we know about Shang rulers comes from studying their tombs. The Shang's belief in ancestor worship and in the existence of an afterlife made them think very carefully about what people would need to have with them when they passed from this life to the next. This was especially important for kings. When a Shang king died, many useful objects such as weapons, tools, pottery, and bronze vessels were buried with him. Dogs were buried with him to protect him in the afterlife. Many of his human subjects were buried with him, too, often while they were still alive! These people were soldiers, servants, slaves, and possibly prisoners of the Shang's many wars. Members of the royal family were sometimes buried with the king as well. The Shang believed that the people who served the king during his life would continue to serve him in the next world.

This illustration shows a Shang royal tomb that could hold the many soldiers, servants, and horses buried with the king.

MANDATE OF HEAVEN: EARLY ZHOU DYNASTY

Though the Shang kings were powerful, their dynasty did not last. Around 1050 BCE, King Wu, the leader of the Zhou province, rebelled against the Shang king and established the Zhou dynasty. The Zhou people believed in a supreme god called Tian, which means Heaven. They believed that Tain wanted them to take control of the kingdom because the Shang ruler was immoral and did not deserve to rule. The Zhou kings were called "Sons of Heaven" and believed that they ruled with the blessing of their god. The idea that their god gave rulers permission to rule was called a Mandate of Heaven and influenced the way the Zhou kings ruled their kingdom. To justify his authority, the king had to behave morally and make decisions that benefited the people of the kingdom. Rule was handed down from father to son, but the son was allowed to rule only if he was considered virtuous enough.

武王

受天眷命　継志前人
遵迩悦豫　偃武修文
惟覧是寶　法度彰明
建用皇極　愛叙彜倫

Zhou king Wu, who overthrew the Shang dynasty and established the Zhou dynasty, was considered a good and just ruler.

UNITED TERRITORIES

During the first years of the Zhou dynasty, the Zhou ruled only the western part of China. Their territory was made up of two hundred separate states that were united under one Zhou king. Like the Shang king, the Zhou ruler served as both priest and king. The priestly role was particularly important for the Zhou king because if crops failed or rivers flooded, the people might think that their king had lost the Mandate of Heaven and use that as a reason to revolt.

The Zhou enjoyed literature and the arts, and they studied astronomy and philosophy, built roads for trade, and developed new technologies, such as the ox-drawn plow. But they also kept large, powerful armies with bronze war chariots to put down revolts and fight off the warlike tribes that frequently invaded from the northwest. Eventually the Zhou were forced to move their capital farther east to be safe from these tribes.

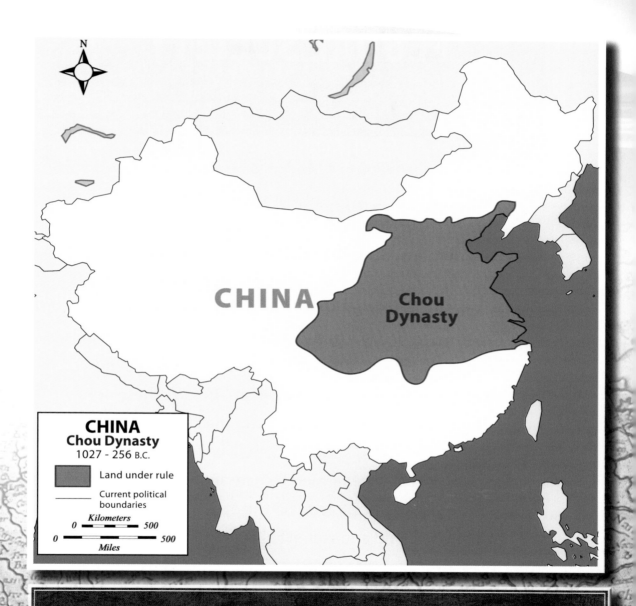

CHINA
Chou Dynasty
1027 - 256 B.C.

Land under rule

Current political boundaries

Kilometers
0   500

0   500
Miles

The Eastern Zhou (sometimes spelled Chou) retreated to a smaller portion of eastern China to avoid the warlike tribes who invaded from the north.

FEUDAL SOCIETY

Zhou society was organized similarly to the feudal systems that became common in Europe many centuries later. The kingdom was divided into states ruled by representatives of the king (usually individuals related to him either by blood or marriage). In exchange for land to rule, these representatives were expected to be loyal to the king. They provided the king with laborers for big construction projects, such as irrigation or roads, and soldiers for military campaigns. In turn, these nobles would often subdivide their land among their own relatives and followers. These large tracts of land were then divided into smaller plots, which were farmed by peasants. Each peasant family worked a specific plot, but in the early Zhou dynasty they did not own their land and weren't allowed to sell what they grew. They were allowed to keep only enough to feed their families. The rest was given to the noble who owned the land.

八駿巡遊

This painting on silk, depicting a Zhou ruler riding in a bronze chariot, is now at the Bibliotheque Nationale in France.

During the early years of the Zhou dynasty, the nobles were very wealthy and lived in luxury, usually within walled cities. The peasants were extremely poor and lived outside the cities in bamboo or mud huts. In the winter when the growing season was over, the peasants often did other jobs for the nobles who owned the land. They might help repair the buildings or roads and frequently served in the lower ranks of the army as well.

In addition to the peasants, Zhou society was made up of commoners who were artisans, servants, or slaves. Artisans might work as blacksmiths, woodworkers, or bronze workers. Some commoners would live and work as household servants in the palaces of the nobles. The Zhou had stopped the Shang practice of consulting oracle bones, so priests, who had helped the Shang rulers with divination, became scribes and scholars in the Zhou dynasty.

This bronze vase, in the shape of an elephant, is from the Zhou dynasty. It was probably used in religious rituals or ceremonies.

KING'S HELPERS

The nobles also helped the Zhou king administer his kingdom. The Zhou king ruled from the main capital city, but the government was spread among many regional cities. The king, therefore, depended on his representatives to administer regional capitals for him in a complex system of bureaucracy. Zhou nobles were given positions of power within the regional capitals, as well as land and portions of the harvest. In exchange, the nobles were charged with administering the regional government and overseeing production on their lands. In this way, the Zhou king was able to rule a widespread and increasingly complex society. As more and more decisions were made by the leaders of the outlying states, however, these nobles became less like representatives of the king and more rulers of their own states. They also had increasingly large armies who were more loyal to them than they were to the king.

Bronze swords like this one were commonly used by the armies raised by the nobles of the Zhou dynasty.

SPRING AND AUTUMN PERIOD: THE LATE ZHOU

The years between 770 BCE and 476 BCE, toward the end of the Zhou dynasty, are called the Spring and Autumn period. This was a prosperous time for much of China. As power became less centralized and the ruling structure changed, so did the social structure. Social classes become much more changeable. Farmers, merchants, and craftsmen were treated with more respect, and commoners were allowed to do jobs that had previously been done only by nobility. For the first time, people were valued for their abilities rather than their family connections.

Under the new system, taxes were determined based on the amount of land one owned, and famers often owned their own plots of land. Farmers were happier during this period since they could keep or sell what remained of their crop after paying taxes. This system also increased revenue for the kingdom and helped create a thriving merchant class.

This bronze cooking vessel was found in Fu Hao's tomb. The techniques used to make this and other similar vessels took a great deal of time and skill.

WAR WITHIN

People in China still speak of the peace and prosperity of the Spring and Autumn period, but the good times did not last. The many provinces that were ruled by nobles eventually began to fight among themselves. The nobles now had large armies, plenty of land, and resources of their own. They were no longer dependent on the king, and so, they did not need to put the king's interests ahead of their own. Not only were they no longer loyal to the king, they also had no reason to be loyal to each other. Many wars broke out between these states and groups of states. This time in China's history is called the Warring States period. In the end, the leader of the strongest of the states took over and supplanted the Zhou leader, beginning the next series of dynasties that lasted through the Imperial period.

This is one of fifty-six ancient tombs from the Warring States period that were found when builders were excavating a construction site in modern-day Zhengzhou, China.

SCHOLARS AND THE FUTURE

The later years of the Zhou dynasty are known as the time of the One Hundred Schools. During this period, philosophers in China began to teach new beliefs and new ways of organizing government and society. The most important of these schools of thought are Confucianism and Legalism. Confucius, the founder of Confucianism, taught that people were basically good and that sticking to traditional values and rituals would create a successful society. Children should respect their parents, and people should respect their leaders. However, Confucius also said that parents must be responsible to their children and governments to their subjects. These teachings were very important in maintaining stable governments during the Warring States period.

According to Legalism, people were not basically good and a strong system of laws was needed to keep order in society. This belief supported a strong bureaucracy in which ability rather than social status determined a person's role in society.

Confucius is remembered and respected even today. Chinese and foreign tourists still visit this statue of Confucius in modern-day Beijing, China.

GLOSSARY

artisan A skilled worker who makes things by hand.

bronze A metal made by combining copper and tin to make an alloy.

Bronze Age A period in early human civilization, following the Stone Age, when tools were made from bronze.

bureaucracy A system of government or organization in which many people make decisions at different levels in the organization.

divination A method of predicting the future or seeking advice by consulting with spirits or supernatural beings.

dynasty A ruling system in which power passes down through families.

feudal A government system in which nobles are granted land in exchange for loyalty and service to the king.

hierarchy A system in which members are organized according to rank based on their status in society or the group.

intercede To ask for assistance on behalf of another person.

mandate The permission or blessing given to one's actions by another.

millet A nutritious grain that grows well in poor soil.

monsoon A seasonal wind that brings heavy rains.

oracle An object or person through which divine or supernatural messages are sought and received.

ore A rock from which metals or minerals can be extracted.

petition To make a formal request or appeal to another.

school of thought An organized system of philosophy, belief, or principles.

scribe In a society that does not have printing, someone who writes documents and keeps records.

silt Soil and sand that is deposited on the bottom of a river or left on land after floodwaters have receded.

Stone Age The earliest known period of human culture, before the Bronze Age, in which tools and implements were made of stone.

The Freeman Spogli Institute for International Studies/Stanford
    Program on International and Cross-cultural Education (SPICE)
616 Serra Street, C100
Stanford University
Stanford, CA 94305-6055
(650) 723-4581
Website: https://spice.fsi.stanford.edu
SPICE offers educational material and programs on a variety of topics,
    including ancient China.

The Institute for Chinese Studies
The Ohio State University
314 Oxley Hall
1712 Neil Avenue
Columbus, OH 43210
(614) 247-6893
Email: china@osu.edu
Website: https://easc.osu.edu/ics
The Institute for Chinese Studies at Ohio State University is a center
    for scholarly research, student training, and public education. ICS
    focuses on the dissemination of knowledge about the cultures,
    languages, history, politics, economies, and educational institu-
    tions of the Chinese-speaking world.

The Metropolitan Museum of Art
1000 5th Avenue
New York, NY 10028
(212) 535-7710
Website: http://www.metmuseum.org/research/metpublications/Ancient_Chinese_Art_The_Ernest_Erickson_Collection_in_The_Metropolitan_Museum_of_Art#about_the_title
The Metropolitan Museum of Art's Ernest Erickson collection contains artwork from Neolithic China through the T'ang period.

San Diego Chinese Historical Museum
404 Third Avenue
San Diego, CA 92101
(619) 338-9888
Website: http://www.sdchm.org
The San Diego Chinese Historical Museum offers regular exhibits, lectures, and programs dealing with the culture and history of China.

WEBSITES

Because of the changing nature of Internet links, Rosen Publishing has developed an online list of websites related to the subject of this book. This site is updated regularly. Please use this link to access the list:

http://www.rosenlinks.com/SRFAC/cgov

FOR FURTHER READING

Burgan, Michael. *Confucius: Chinese Philosopher and Teacher*. North Mankato, MN: Compass Point, 2008.

Clarke, Ginjer L. *What's Up in the Gobi Desert*. New York, NY: Grosset and Dunlap, 2016.

Friedman, Mel. *Ancient China*. New York, NY: Scholastic, 2010.

Greenberger, Robert. *The Technology of Ancient China*. New York, NY: Rosen, 2006.

Kramer, Lance. *Great Ancient China Projects You Can Build Yourself*. White River Junction, VT: Nomad Press, 2008.

O'Connor, Jane. *The Emperor's Silent Army: Terracotta Warriors of Ancient China*. New York, NY: Viking Books for Young Readers, 2002.

Ransom, Candice. *Tools and Treasures of Ancient China*. Minneapolis, MN: Lerner, 2014.

Roberts, Russell. *Ancient China*. Newark, DE: Mitchell Lane, 2013.

Rosinsky, Natalie M. *Ancient China*. North Mankato, MN: Compass Point, 2013.

Shepherd, Aaron. *The Monkey King: A Superhero Tale of China*. Friday Harbor, WA: Skyhook Press, 2008.

Strapp, James. *Inside Ancient China* (Science and Technology). New York, NY: Routledge, 2009.

Ting, Renee. *Chinese History Stories, Vol 1: Stories from the Zhou Dynasty*. Walnut Creek, CA: Shen's Books, 2009.

BIBLIOGRAPHY

"Ancient Civilizations." Independence Hall Association, Philadelphia, 2014. Retrieved November 2015 (http://www.ushistory.org/civ/9b.asp).

Boehm, Richard G., et al. *Ancient Civilizations*. New York, NY: Harcourt Brace, 2002.

City University of New York. "Chinese Cultural Studies." 1995. Retrieved November 2015 (http://acc6.its.brooklyn.cuny.edu/~phalsall/texts/chinhist.html).

Columbia University. "Asia for Educators." 2009. Retrieved November 2015 (http://afe.easia.columbia.edu/main_pop/kpct/index.html#kp1)

Duiker, William J., and Jackson J. Spielvogel. *World History*. Belmont, CA: Wadsworth, 2001.

Ebrey, Patricia Buckley. "A Visual Sourcebook of Chinese Civilization." Retrieved November 2015 (http://depts.washington.edu/chinaciv/index.htm).

Indiana University. "Neolithic China." Retrieved November 2015 (http://www.indiana.edu/~g380/3.7-Neolithic-2010.pdf).

Lai, Selena, and Waka Takahashi Brown. "Shang Dynasty." Stanford University Program on International and Cross-Cultural Education, November 2006. Retrieved November 2015 (http://spice.fsi.stanford.edu/docs/the_shang_dynasty_1600_to_1050_bce).

Loewe, Michael, and Edward Shaughnessy. *The Cambridge History of Ancient China*. Cambridge, MA: Cambridge University Press, 1999.

San Jose State University Department of Economics. "The Spring and Autumn Period of Ancient China." Retrieved November 2015 (http://www.sjsu.edu/faculty/watkins/springautumn.htm).

Spodek, Howard. *The World's History*. Upper Saddle River, NJ: Prentice Hall, 2000.

Taiwan Government. "Artifacts from the Late Shang Dynasty Royal Tomb." National Palace Museum. Retrieved November 2015 (http://www.npm.gov.tw/exhbition/ctom2000/english/etom2000.htm).

University of Maryland. "History of China." Retrieved November, 2015 (http://www.chaos.umd.edu/history).

INDEX

ABOUT THE AUTHOR

Avery Elizabeth Hurt writes articles and books for children and young adults. She has not yet visited China but studies Chinese philosophy and drinks huge amounts of Chinese tea—preferably from Yunnan province.

PHOTO CREDITS